Anthems
for SA & Men

9 anthems for sopranos,
altos, and unison men

MUSIC DEPARTMENT

OXFORD
UNIVERSITY PRESS

Great Clarendon Street, Oxford OX2 6DP,
United Kingdom

Oxford University Press is a department of the University of Oxford.
It furthers the University's objective of excellence in research, scholarship,
and education by publishing worldwide. Oxford is a registered trade mark of
Oxford University Press in the UK and in certain other countries

First published 2018

Impression: 1

ISBN 978-0-19-352417-0

Music and text origination by
Katie Johnston
Printed in Great Britain on acid-free paper by
Halstan & Co. Ltd, Amersham, Bucks.

Contents

Alleluia, sing to Jesus!

William Chatterton Dix (adap.)
(1837–98)

ALAN SMITH
(1962–2017)

Duration: 3 mins

Also published separately in a version for SATB and organ (ISBN 978–0–19–339568–8). This version has been prepared by Alan Bullard.

13
Hark, the songs of peace-ful Si - on Thun-der like a might - y flood;
Man.
17
Je - sus, out of ev - 'ry na - tion, has re - deemed us by his
Ped.
21
blood.
mp
Al - le-
mf
sim.
Man.

25
-lu - ia, not_ as or - phans Are we left in sor - row now,_ Al-le-
mp
Ped.
29
-lu - ia, he_ is near_ us, Faith be-lieves, nor ques - tions how:
3
33
mf
Though the cloud from sight re-ceived him When the for - ty days were o'er,
mf
Man.

37
mf
Shall our hearts for - get his pro - mise, 'I am with you ev - er -
Ped.
mp
Man.
41
p
-more'?
p
più legato
45
mp
Al - le - lu - ia, bread of an - gels, Here on earth our food and stay;

49
mp
Al - le - lu - ia, here the sin - ful_ Flee to you from day_ to_ day.
53
In - ter - ces - sor, friend of sin - ners, Earth's Re - deem - er, plead for_ me,_
all the sin - less Sweep a-cross the cry - stal
57
Where the songs of all the_ sin - less Sweep a - cross the cry - stal

61
unis. f
sea.
Al-le - lu - ia, King e- ter - nal The
f
Ped.
f
65
Lord of lords we own;
Al-le - lu - ia, born of Ma - ry, Earth your
sim.
69
foot - stool, hea-ven your throne:
You with-in the veil have en - tered, Robed in

73
flesh, our great high priest;
You on earth both priest and Sa - viour
77
In the Eu - cha - ris - - - tic feast.
82
rall.
sim.
rall.
ff

Bless to me this day

St Brendan the Voyager (484–577)
from *Carmina Gadelica*, Vol. III (1940)

CECILIA McDOWALL
(b. 1951)

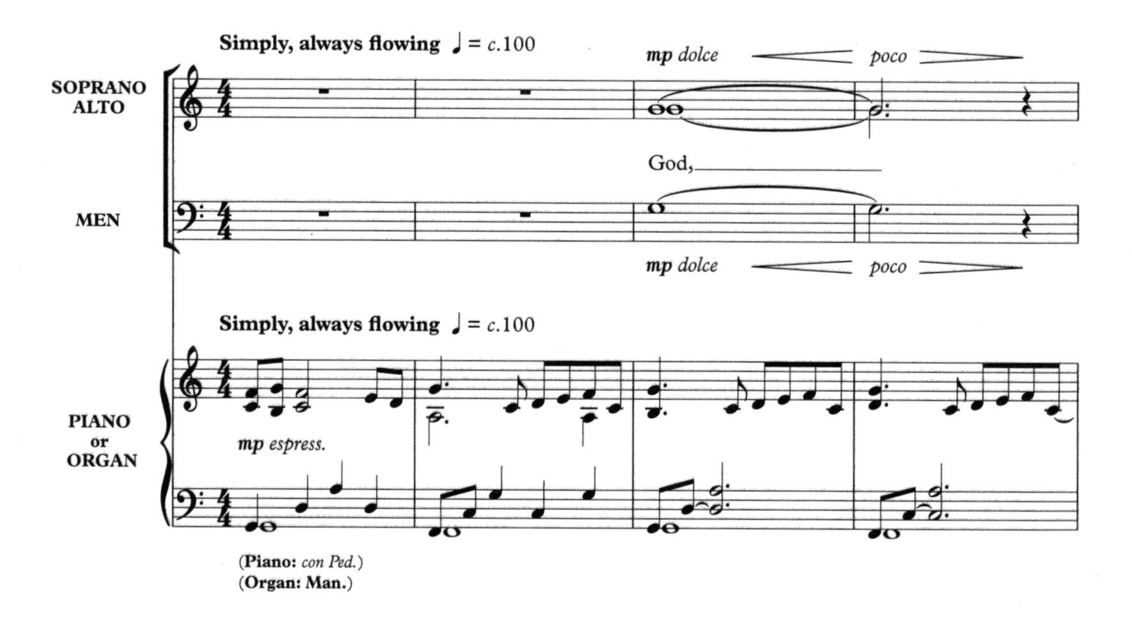

Duration: 4 mins

Also published separately in a version for SA and piano/organ (ISBN 978–0–19–338621–1).

mp
mf
bless this day,
bless this day,
(Ped.)
p
God,
bless to me,
bless
bless
this
this night,
bless
this
f

pochiss. rit.
20
mf
S.
— night, this night;
Bless, O
A.
night, this night;
Bless, O
M.
night, this night;
pochiss. rit.

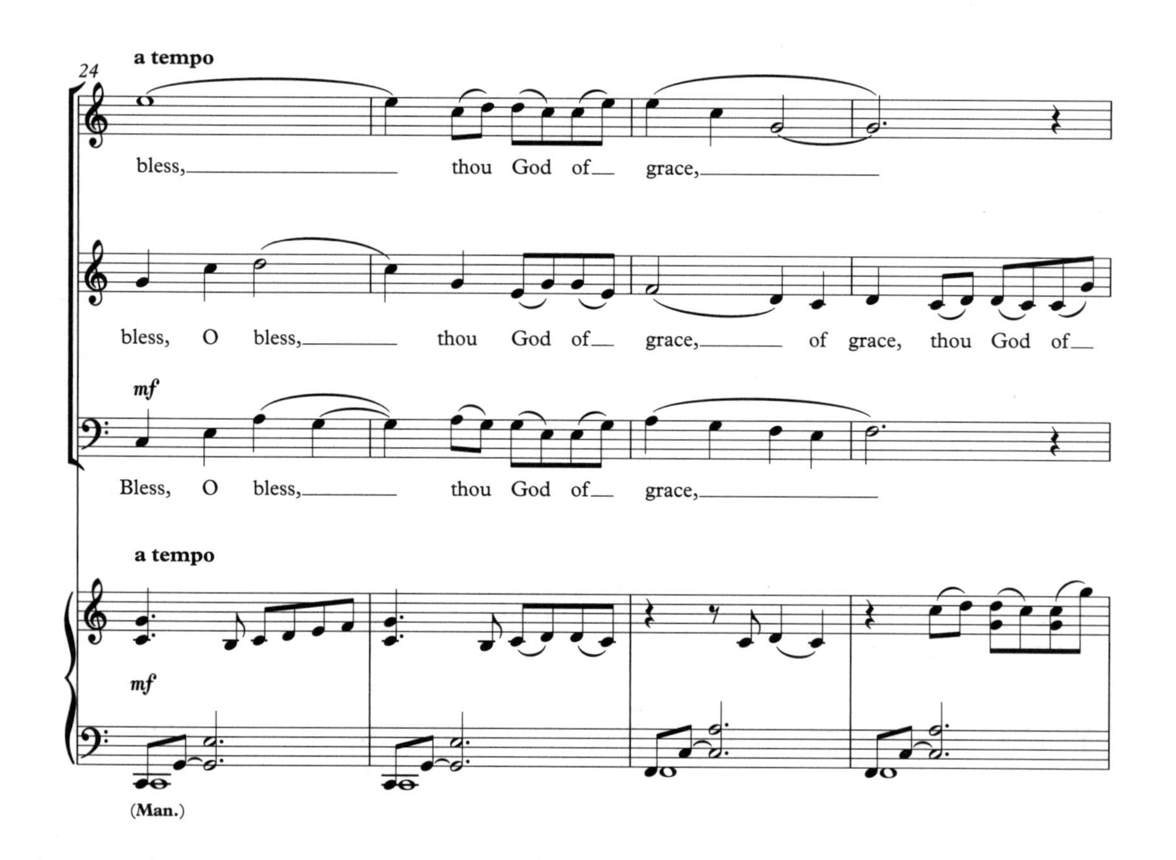
24
a tempo
bless, thou God of grace,
bless, O bless, thou God of grace, of grace, thou God of
mf
Bless, O bless, thou God of grace,
a tempo
mf
(Man.)

28
f
Each day and hour of my life, of life.
grace, Each hour of my life, of my life.
Each day and hour of my life, of life.

32
mp
mf
O bless, O bless, thou God,
O bless, O bless, thou God, thou God of grace,
Bless, thou God, thou God of grace,

36
mp
mf
Each day and hour of my life.
Each day and hour of my life, of my life.
mp
mf
legato
f

41
mp
poco
God, bless the
God, bless the

* Small notes indicate optional *divisi.*

54
p
mp
God,
bless the earth that is be-
bless the earth,
bless the earth be-
God,
bless the earth, the earth that is be-
mp
(Man.)

57
mf
f
-neath my sole, God, bless the earth, the
-neath my sole, God, bless the earth, the
-neath my sole, God, bless the earth, the

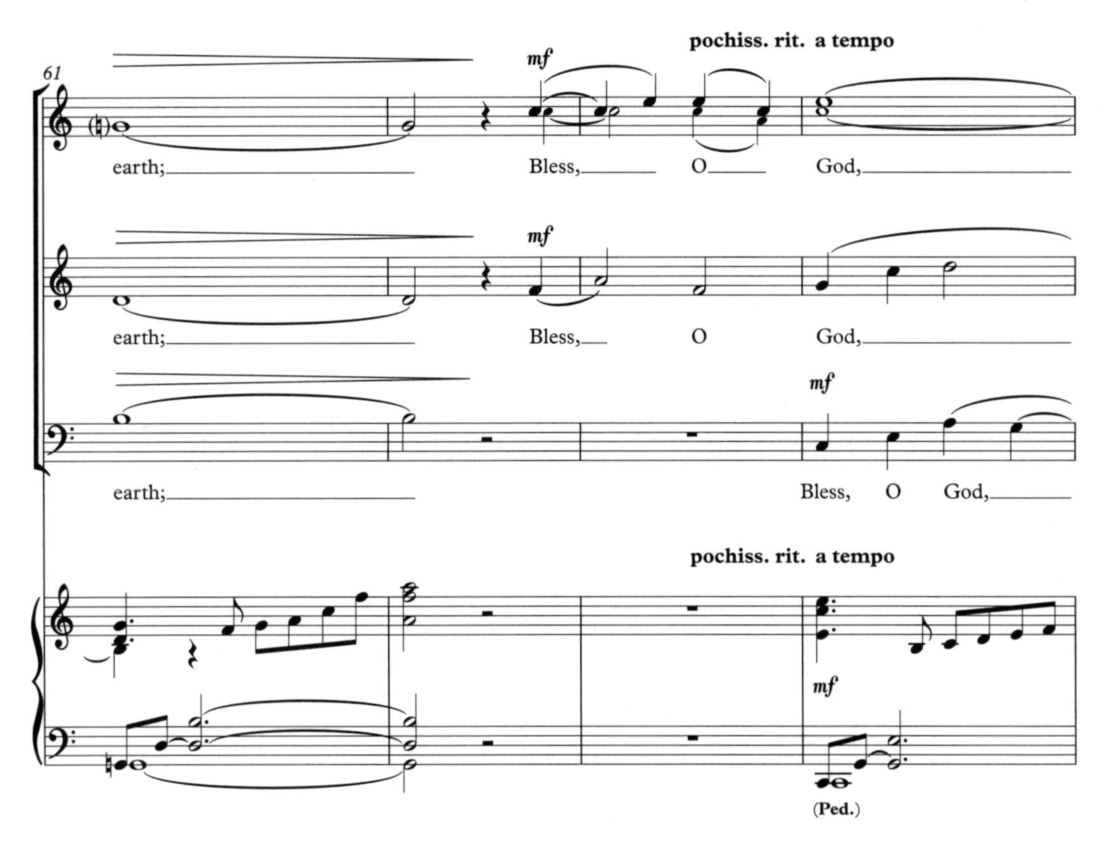
pochiss. rit. a tempo
mf
earth;
Bless, O God,
mf
earth;
Bless, O God,
mf
earth;
Bless, O God,
pochiss. rit. a tempo
mf
(Ped.)

and give to me thy love,
O God of
and give to me thy love, give to me thy love,
Of
and give to me thy love,
O God of

69
f
gods, bless my rest and my re-pose;
mp
O bless, O
gods, bless my rest;
O bless, O
gods, bless my rest and my re-pose;
(Man.)

73
mf
mp
God, O bless,
bless my
God, and give to me thy love,
bless my
God, and give to me thy love,
bless my

77
pochiss. rit.
mf
f
rest, my re - pose.
Bless, O
rest, my re - pose, my re - pose.
Bless, O
rest, my re - pose, my re - pose.
pochiss. rit.
(Ped.)

81
a tempo
God, and give to me thy love,
God, and give to me thy love, give to me thy
f
God, and give to me thy love,
a tempo
f
(Ped.)

85
O God of gods, bless my rest and my re-pose,
love, Of gods, bless my rest,
O God of gods, bless my rest and my re-pose,

89
mf
mp
And bless, O God, and bless, O God,
And bless, O God of gods, and bless, O God of gods,
And bless, O God, and bless, O God,

93
dim. poco a poco
and_ bless, O God, my re - pose,
dim. poco a poco
and bless, O_ God of gods, my re - pose,_
dim. poco a poco
and bless, O_ God, my re - pose,
dim. poco a poco

ritardando
97
pp
my re - pose, re - pose._
pp
my re - pose._
pp
my re - pose, re - pose._
ritardando
pp

Faith, hope, and love remain

1 Corinthians 13: 13 and Song of Solomon 8: 6–7

MALCOLM ARCHER
(b. 1952)

Duration: 4 mins

Also published in versions for SATB and organ (ISBN 978–0–19–338924–3), and SA and organ/piano (ISBN 978–0–19–340165–5).

12
faith, hope, and love, faith, hope, and
(Man.)
15
cresc.
mf
love, but the great - est of these is love, but the
cresc.
(Ped.)
18
great - est of these is love.
mf
21
MEN mf
M.
And now these three re - main:

24
faith, hope, and love,
faith, hope, and

27
f
mf
love, but the great - est of these is love, but the

30
S.
A.
M.
For
S. mf
A.
mf For love is strong as
mf
great - est of these is love.
For

33
death, is strong as death,
strong as
36
death,
strong as death.
f
Ma-ny
f
39
mf
mp
wa - ters can-not quench love,
nei - ther can the floods
mf
mp

43
p
drown it,
drown it.
p
mp
47
poco rall.
a tempo
mp
And now these three re-main:
mp
poco rall.
a tempo
51
faith, hope, and love,
faith, hope, and

54
mf
f
love, but the great - est of these is love, but the
mf
f
f
57
ff
f
these
great - est of is love, is
these, the great - est of these
ff
f
(Tuba)
ff
poco rall.
60
mf
love, but the great - est of these is
mf
poco rall.
f
mf

a tempo
63
mp
love.
mp
a tempo
mp
(Man.)
66
70
rall.
rall.
p
(Ped.)

Fill your hearts with joy and gladness

Timothy Dudley-Smith
(b. 1926)

SARAH QUARTEL
(b. 1982)

Duration: c.2 mins

Also published in a version for flexible voices in *The Oxford Book of Easy Flexible Anthems* (ISBN 978–0–19–341325–2).

* The keyboard part may be omitted in verse 3, entering in bar 29.

25
mf
grass up-on the moun-tain pas-tures, gold-en val - leys thick with grain.
mf
mf
tenuto
a tempo
29
SOPRANOS
f
4. Fill your hearts with joy and
ALTOS & MEN
f
4. Fill your hearts with joy and glad - ness,
tenuto
a tempo
mf
f
(Ped.)
32
glad - ness, with joy and glad - ness, de - clare his judg-ments,
peace and plen - ty crown your days; love his laws, de - clare his judg-ments,

36
walk in his words and ways; he the
walk in all his words and ways; he the Lord and
39
rit. al fine
ff
Lord and we his child - ren: praise the Lord, the Lord,
we his child - ren: praise the Lord, all peo - ple, praise the Lord, all peo - ple,
rit. al fine
ff
42
praise the Lord, all peo - ple, praise!
praise the Lord, all peo - ple, praise!
(Pno RH)

From the break of the day

Jan Struther
(1901–53)

ALAN BULLARD
(b. 1947)

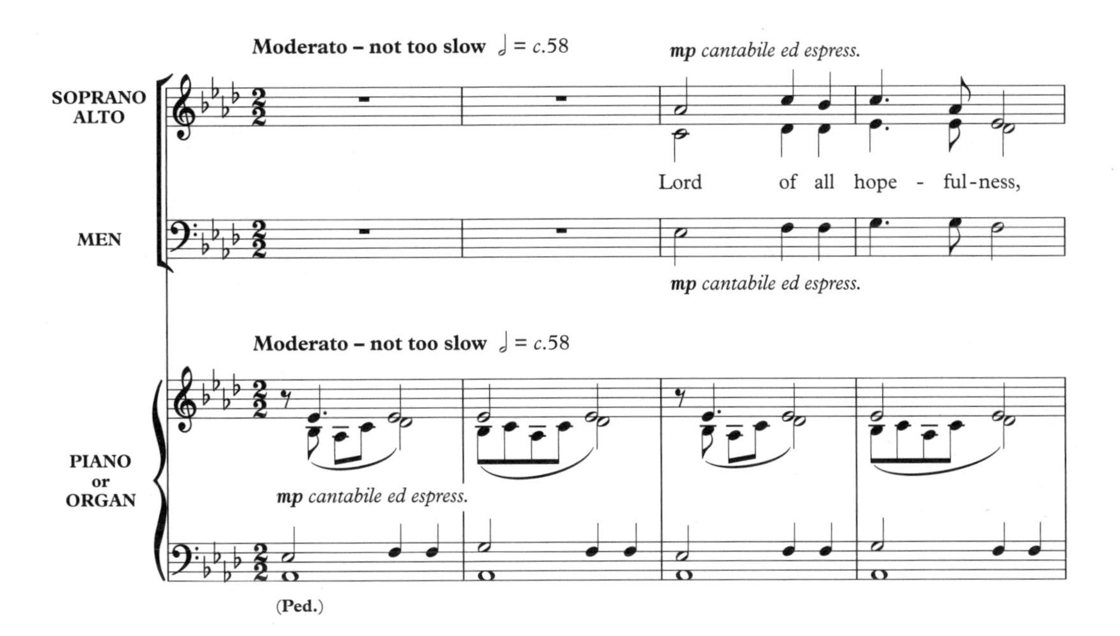

Duration: c.3 mins

Also published in a version for SATB and piano/organ, available separately (ISBN 978–0–19–337141–5) and in *Alan Bullard Anthems* (ISBN 978–0–19–336931–3).

9
cares could de - stroy.
mf
cares could de - stroy.
Be there at our wak - ing,
cares could de - stroy.
mf
mf
13
and give us, we pray, Your bliss in our hearts, Lord,
17
p
at the break of the day.
p
p

21
mf brighter
mp
faith,
Whose
Lord of all ea - ger-ness,
Lord of all faith,
mf brighter
mp
faith,
Whose
mf brighter
mp
mf brighter
mp
25
strong hands were skilled at the plane and the lathe,
mf
Whose hands were skilled at the plane and the lathe,
mf
strong hands were skilled at the plane and the lathe,
mf
29
Be there at our la - bours and give us, we pray, Your
cresc.
Be there at our la - bours and give us, we pray, Your
cresc.
Be there at our la - bours, give us, we pray, Your
cresc.

strength in our
strength in our hearts, Lord, at the noon of the day.
strength in our
p gently
Lord of all kind - li-ness, Lord of all
p gently
(Man.)
ALTOS
p gently
Your hands swift to wel - come, your arms to em-
grace,
mp

45
mp cresc.
S.
A.
-brace, Be there_ at our hom - ing, and
cresc.
Be_ there at our hom - ing, and
cresc.
(Ped.)
give us, we_ pray, Your love in our hearts,_ Lord,
mf pp p
48
give us, we_ pray, Your love in our hearts, at the
mf pp p
give_ us, we pray, Your love in our hearts, at the
mf pp p
at the eve_ of the day._
poco rit.
52
eve of the day._
eve_ of the day._
poco rit.

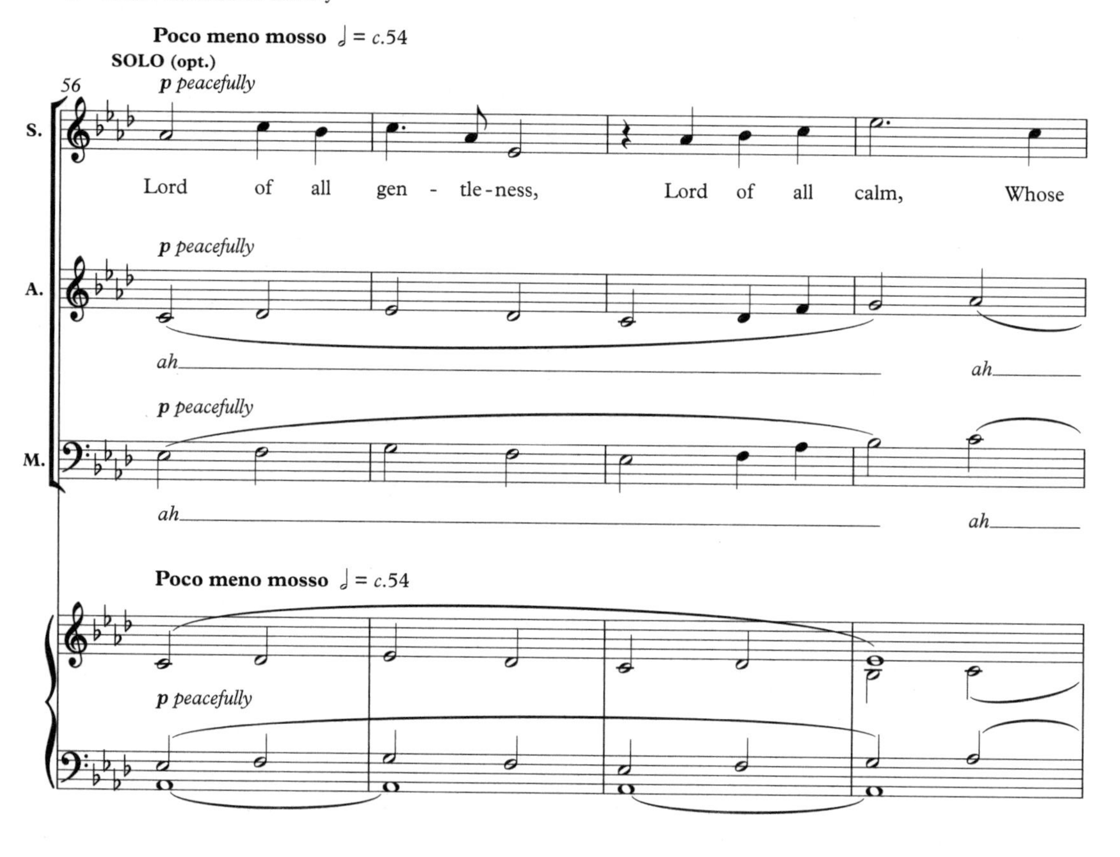
Poco meno mosso 𝅗𝅥 = c.54
SOLO (opt.)
56
p peacefully
S.
Lord of all gen - tle-ness, Lord of all calm, Whose
p peacefully
A.
ah ah
p peacefully
M.
ah ah
Poco meno mosso 𝅗𝅥 = c.54
p peacefully

60
voice is con - tent - ment, whose pres - ence is balm,

64
(TUTTI)
S.
A.
M.
poco
Be there at our sleep - ing, and give us, we pray, Your
68
p
peace in our hearts, Lord, at the end of the day,
72
meno mosso
a tempo
pp
poco rit.
at the end of the day.
ppp

I lift my eyes

Timothy Dudley-Smith
(b. 1926)

BOB CHILCOTT
(b. 1955)

Duration: c.4 mins

Also published separately in a version for SSAA and piano (ISBN 978-0-19-337837-7).

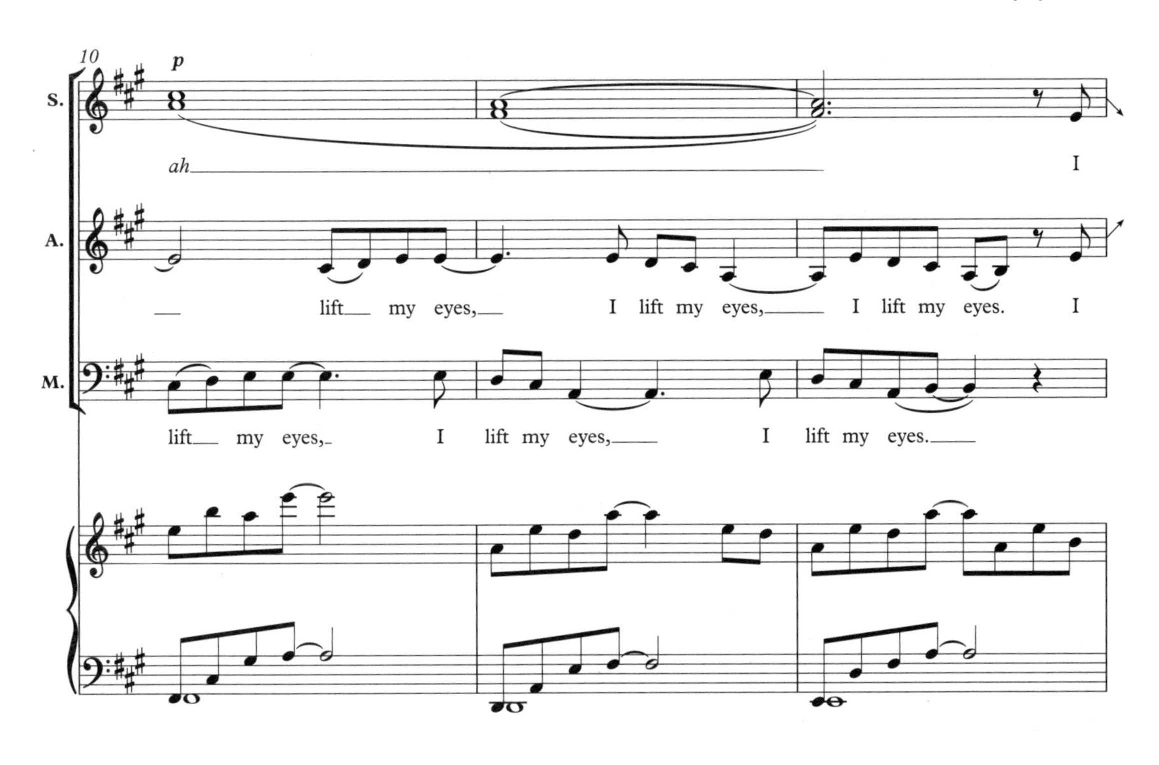
10
p
S.
A.
M.
ah
I
lift my eyes,
I lift my eyes,
I lift my eyes.
I
lift my eyes,
I lift my eyes,
I lift my eyes.

13
unis.
S./A.
lift my eyes to the qui - et hills in the press of a bu - sy day; as

15
green hills stand in a dust - y land so God is my strength and stay.

17
mf ma dolce
I lift my eyes, I
mf ma dolce

20
lift my eyes, I lift my eyes

23
p
S.
A.
to the qui - et hills.
p sost.

27
unis. mp
S./A.
M.
I lift my eyes to the qui - et hills to a
mp
I lift my eyes to the
mp
29
calm that is mine to share; se - cure and still in the Fa - ther's will and
qui - et hills to a calm that is mine to share; se - cure and still in the
31
S.
A.
M.
kept by the Fa - ther's care. I
kept by the Fa - ther's care.
Fa - ther's will and kept by the Fa - ther's care.

33
mf ma dolce
lift my eyes, I lift my eyes,
mf ma dolce
I lift my eyes, I lift
mf ma dolce
I lift my eyes,
mf ma dolce

36
I lift my eyes to the qui - et
my eyes, I lift my eyes to the qui - et
I lift my eyes to the qui - et

39
mp
mf
S.
A.
hills.
I lift my eyes to the qui-
M.
mp
mf
mp
mf
42
-et hills with a prayer as I turn to sleep;
by
45
day, by night, through the dark and light my

47
Shep-herd will guard his sheep.
50
S./A.
p sost.
S./A. unis. p
I
54
lift my eyes to the qui - et hills and my heart to the Fa - ther's throne; in
56
all my ways to the end of days the Lord will pre-serve his own.

mf ma dolce
I lift my eyes, I
mf ma dolce

lift my eyes, I lift my eyes

S.
A.
to the qui - et hills.
I

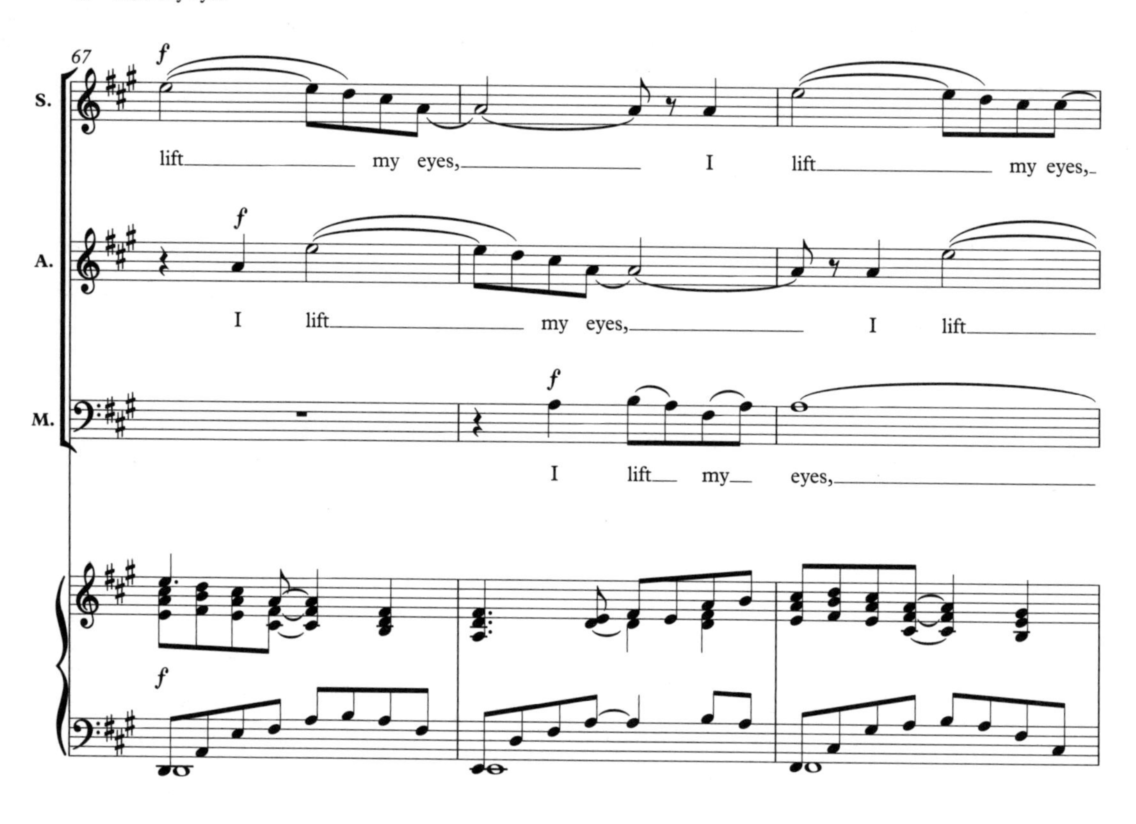
67
S.
f
lift my eyes, I lift my eyes,
A.
f
I lift my eyes, I lift
M.
f
I lift my eyes,
f

70
I lift my eyes to the qui - et
my eyes, I lift my eyes to the qui - et
I lift my eyes to the qui - et

73
p
hills.
p
hills.
p
hills.
p sost.
77
ALTOS p
A.
Lift my eyes,
lift my eyes,
I lift my eyes,
80
S.
p
ah
A.
I lift my eyes.
Lift my eyes,
lift my eyes,
M.
p
Lift my eyes,
lift my eyes,
I

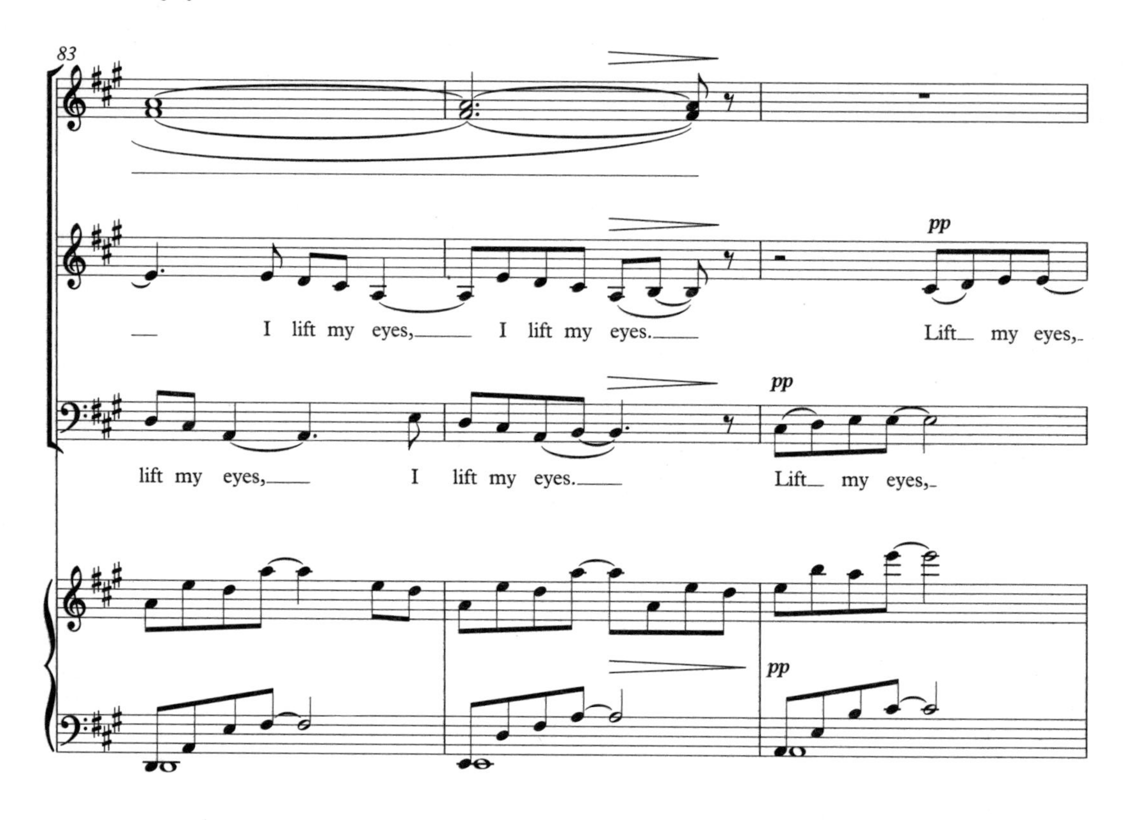
83
pp
I lift my eyes, I lift my eyes. Lift my eyes,
pp
lift my eyes, I lift my eyes. Lift my eyes,
pp

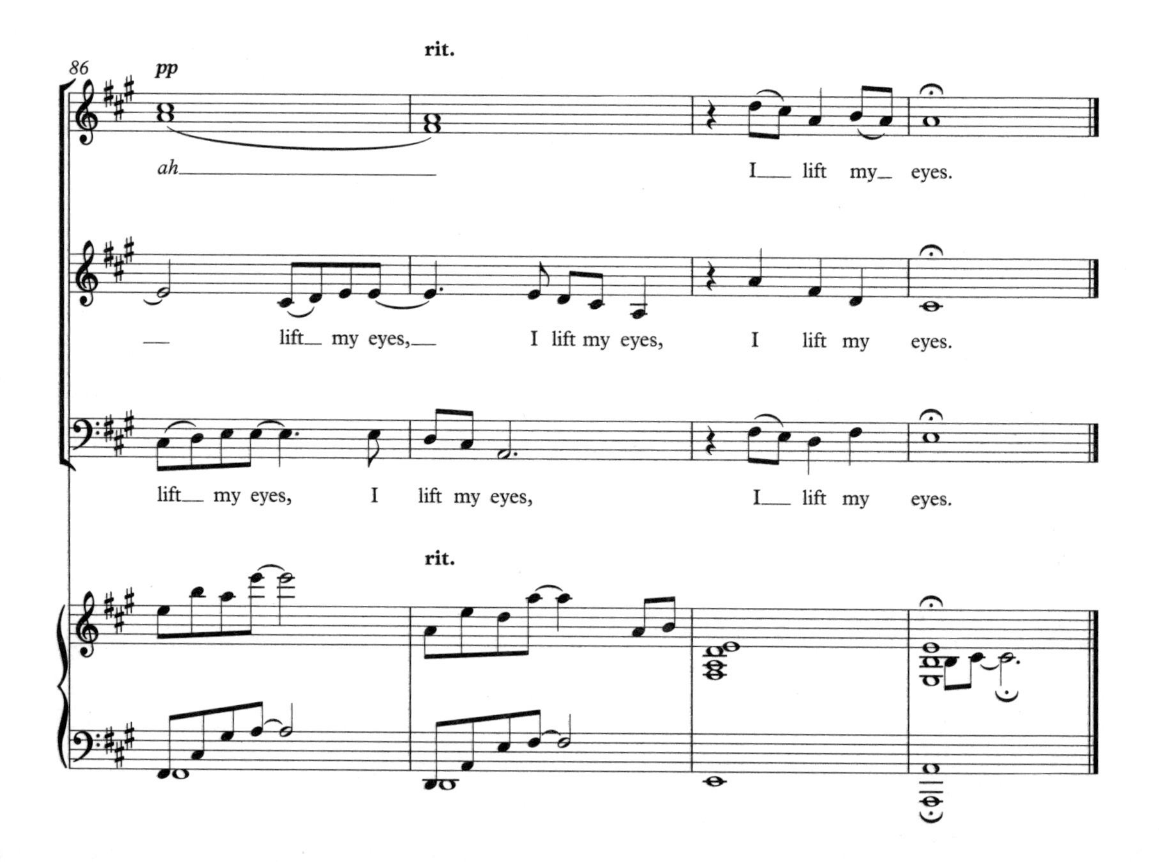
86
pp
rit.
ah
I lift my eyes.
lift my eyes, I lift my eyes, I lift my eyes.
lift my eyes, I lift my eyes, I lift my eyes.
rit.

O God, you speak your beauty every hour

Words and music by
HOWARD HELVEY
'MARCUM'

Duration: c.4 mins

Also published separately in a version for SATB and organ (ISBN 978-0-19-341273-6).

9
mp
O God, you speak your beau - ty ev - 'ry
3
13
S./A. unis. mp
In
hour, from soar - ing peaks to val - leys fed by springs.
3
17
ev - 'ry liv - ing soul and fra - grant flow'r your han - di -

21
mf
-work is seen— cre-a - tion sings!
As peo - ple in your
mf
mf
25
unis.
im - age, we a - spire and live to mir - ror your cre -
3
3
3
29
mp
- a - tive fire.
mp
mp (reduce)

* If necessary, the organ may lightly double the choral parts from b. 37 to b. 55.

45
hand we move from depths be - low to heights a -
49
mp
grace ex -
-bove. May we, with hearts up - lift - ed by your grace, ex -
mp
53
-tend your
mf
-tend your love to ev - 'ry land and race.
mf
mf
(Man.)
mf
Ped.
57
3
3
(add)

62
poco rit.
3
cresc.

poco meno mosso ♩ = c.96
66
SOPRANOS
f
O Spi - rit, giv - ing breath to all the earth, we
ALTOS & MEN
f
O Spi - rit, giv - ing breath to all the earth, we
poco meno mosso ♩ = c.96
f

70
grow in faith and strength from your clear flame. O Wind of Heav'n, re-
grow in faith and strength from your clear flame. O Wind of Heav'n, re -

74
-called at our re - birth, the world a-waits the u -
-called at our re - birth, the world a - waits the
78
- ni - ty we claim. With zeal we strive, as - sist - ed by your
u - ni-ty we claim. With zeal we strive, as - sist - ed by your
82
poco rit.
might, to fill the earth with ev - er - last - ing
might, to fill the earth with ev - er - last - ing
poco rit.

a tempo
poco rit.
Light.
Light.
a tempo
poco rit.
poco meno mosso ♩ = c.92
più f
S.
A.
We'll fill the earth with ev - er - last -
M.
più f
poco meno mosso ♩ = c.92
più f
allargando
- ing Light.
allargando

Praise the Lord, ye heavens adore him

Anon., from *Foundling Hospital Collection*, 1796/1801 (altd)
Based on Psalm 148: 1–6, 14

ALAN BULLARD
(b. 1947)

With life and spirit ♩ = *c.*120

SOPRANO ALTO

MEN

unis. ***f***

Praise the

f

With life and spirit ♩ = *c.*120

ORGAN or PIANO

f

(Ped.)

5

Lord, ye heav'ns a - dore him; Praise him, an - gels in the height; Sun and

9

moon, bow down be - fore him, Praise him, all ye stars and light. Praise the

Duration: *c.*2 mins

Also published separately in a version for SATB and organ/piano (ISBN 978-0-19-339567-1).

13
Lord, for he hath spo - ken; Worlds his might - y voice o - beyed; And
17
laws, that ne - ver shall be bro - ken, For their guid - ance he hath
21
made.

25
p legato
Praise him, an - gels in the
mp
Praise the Lord, ye heav'ns a - dore him; Praise him, an - gels in the
p
29
height; Praise him, all ye stars and
height; Sun and moon, bow down be - fore him, Praise him, all ye stars and
33
mf
light. Praise the Lord, for he is glo - rious; Ne - ver shall his pro-mise
mf
light. Praise the Lord, praise the
mf

* small notes optional

50
an - gels in the height; Sun and moon, bow down be - fore him, Praise him,
54
ff
all ye stars and light. Praise the God of our sal - va - tion; An - gel
ff
all ye stars, praise him, all ye stars and light. Praise the God of our sal -
ff
58
hosts his pow'r pro - claim; For heav'n and earth, and all cre - a - tion,
-va - tion; An - gel hosts his pow'r pro - claim; For heav'n and earth, and

* optional Soprano *divisi*

This day

Jewish text
adap. Bob Chilcott

BOB CHILCOTT
(b. 1955)

Duration: c.2 mins

Also published in a version for SA and piano as part of the larger work, *This Day* (ISBN 978–0–19–335933–8).

mf
This day in-scribe us for a hap-py, hap-py life.
mp
This day hear our cry.
This day, this
This day ac-cept our prayer in
day.
This day, this day.
mer-cy and fa-vour. This day sup-port us with your right-eous hand.

16
This day ac-cept our prayer in mer - cy and fa-vour.
This day, this day.
This day, this
19
day.
dolce
This day, this
This day will you strength us.
mp dolce
22
day.
This day, this day.
This day will you bless us.
This day will you lift us, vi - sit us for good.

25
mf
This day in-scribe us for a hap - py, hap - py, life.
mf
mf

28
mp
S.
This day hear our cry.
espress.
A - men, a -
A.
This day hear our cry.
espress.
A -
M.
This day hear our cry.
espress.
A - men,
mp
espress.

31
mf
-men, a - men, a - men, a -
mf
- men, a - men, a - men, a -
mf
a - men, a - men, a - men, a -
mf

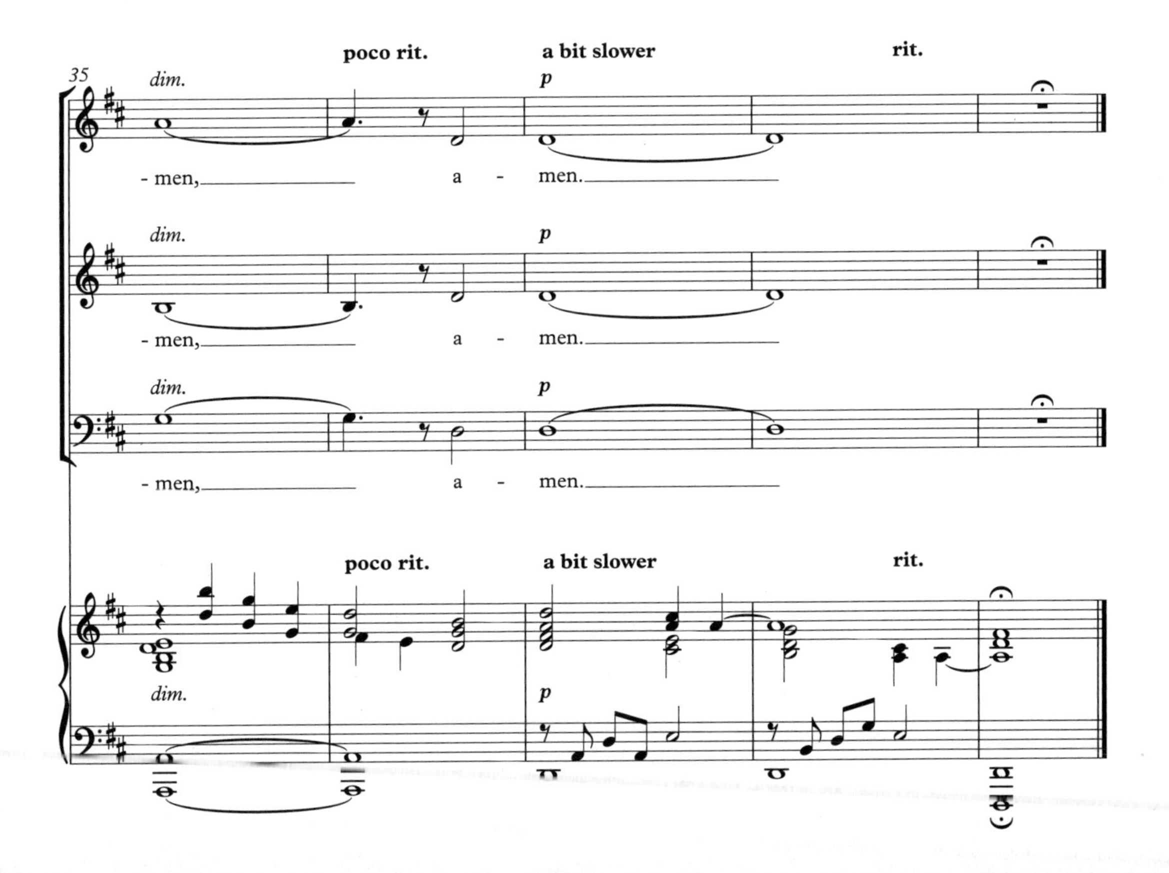
35
poco rit.
a bit slower
rit.
dim.
p
- men, a - men.
dim.
p
- men, a - men.
dim.
p
- men, a - men.
poco rit.
a bit slower
rit.
dim.
p